A Universe of Rainbows

For Lee, the Dear One,
whose colorful spirit continues to inspire our world.

— M. F. E.

For Mom,
who always pointed out parhelia in the sky
and said they were our guardian angels.

— J. C.

Eerdmans Books for Young Readers would like to thank
Jill Holz (B.S. Geology and Geophysics, MEd., and National Geographic Certified Educator)
for sharing her scientific expertise about rainbows in all their forms.

Thanks are due for commissioned works used by permission of the respective authors, who control all rights:
Nikki Grimes for "The Saturday of No"; Matt Forrest Esenwine for "Sun Dogs," "Elegant Danger," "World Beneath Our Feet," "Alien Fountain," and "Jewel of the Pasture";
Renée M. LaTulippe for "Hello, Pilot!"; Joyce Sidman for "Along the Zambezi"; Irene Latham for "The Rainbow Keeper"; David L. Harrison for "Reflections on the Pool";
Alma Flor Ada and F. Isabel Campoy for "Echoes of Rain"; Marilyn Singer for "Rainbows in a Cage"; Charles Ghigna for "Night Gem";
Janet Wong for "If the Mountain Could Talk"; Allan Wolf for "What We Left in Rainbow Cave."

Thanks are also due for "Sing the Life Prismatic" by Heidi E.Y. Stemple and Jane Yolen; "Caño Cristales Speaks" by Amy Ludwig VanDerwater; "Petals of Paradise" by
Rebecca Kai Dotlich; "The Rainbowfish . . ." by Laura Purdie Salas; "The Fruit Fly's Secret" by Lee Wardlaw; "Garden of Stars" by Georgia Heard. Used by permission of
Curtis Brown, Ltd., and the respective authors, who control all rights.

"Lament of the Fruit Farmer" by Charles Waters used by permission of Stimola Literary Studio.

Illustrations © 2025 Jamey Christoph • Published in 2025 by Eerdmans Books for Young Readers, an imprint of Wm. B. Eerdmans Publishing Co., Grand Rapids, Michigan

www.eerdmans.com/youngreaders • All rights reserved • Manufactured in China

34 33 32 31 30 29 28 27 26 25   1 2 3 4 5 6 7 8 9

ISBN 978-0-8028-5571-8 • A catalog record of this book is available from the Library of Congress. • Illustrations created digitally

A Universe of Rainbows

MULTICOLORED POEMS
FOR A MULTICOLORED WORLD

Poems selected by
Matt Forrest Esenwine

Illustrated by
Jamey Christoph

EERDMANS BOOKS FOR YOUNG READERS
GRAND RAPIDS, MICHIGAN

Introduction

A drop of water. Peru's Vinicunca mountain. The star Betelgeuse, in the constellation Orion.

What do they all have in common?

Rainbows!

A drop of water can act as a prism, refracting light into all its colorful glory. Vinicunca, known as Rainbow Mountain, is made up of layers of minerals that create a natural geologic "rainbow." And Betelgeuse, the star most of us know as one of Orion's shoulders, is surrounded by a massive, swirling cloud of gas astronomers call the "Rainbow Nebula."

While rainbows may be symbols of pride, diversity, and hope . . . they are much, much more. They are the brilliance of a tiny diamond, the multicolored feathers of a Gouldian finch, the shimmering waters of the river Caño Cristales in Colombia. Rainbows are everywhere, in all shapes, sizes, and forms—so come discover a world of rainbows, and the poetry they inspire!

Table of Contents

RAINBOWS OF LIGHT

"The Saturday of No"
(Rainbows)

Nikki Grimes

"Sun Dogs"
(Parhelia)

Matt Forrest Esenwine

"Hello, Pilot!"
(Pilot's Glories)

Renée M. LaTulippe

"Along the Zambezi"
(Moonbow)

Joyce Sidman

"The Rainbow Keeper"
(Prisms and Crystals)

Irene Latham

RAINBOW WATERS

"Reflections on the Pool"
(Morning Glory Pool)

David L. Harrison

"Sing the Life Prismatic"
(Grand Prismatic Spring)

Heidi E.Y. Stemple & Jane Yolen

"Alien Fountain"
(Fly Geyser)

Matt Forrest Esenwine

"Caño Cristales Speaks"
(Caño Cristales)

Amy Ludwig VanDerwater

LIVING RAINBOWS

"Echoes of Rain"
(Rainbow Eucalyptus Trees)

Alma Flor Ada & F. Isabel Campoy

"Lament of the Fruit Farmer"
(Rainbow Lorikeet)

Charles Waters

"Rainbows in a Cage"
(Gouldian Finch)

Marilyn Singer

"Petals of Paradise"
(Rainbow Hibiscus)

Rebecca Kai Dotlich

"Elegant Danger"
(Peacock Mantis Shrimp)

Matt Forrest Esenwine

"The Rainbowfish . . ."
(Rainbowfish)

Laura Purdie Salas

"Night Gem"
(Peacock Spider)

Charles Ghigna

"Jewel of the Pasture"
(Rainbow Scarab)

Matt Forrest Esenwine

"The Fruit Fly's Secret"
(Insect Wings)

Lee Wardlaw

RAINBOWS OF ROCK

"If the Mountain Could Talk"
(Vinicunca)

Janet Wong

"What We Left in Rainbow Cave"
(Las Cavernas de Mármol)

Allan Wolf

"World Beneath Our Feet"
(Zhangye Danxia National Geopark)

Matt Forrest Esenwine

RAINBOWS BEYOND

"Garden of Stars"
(Rainbow Nebula)

Georgia Heard

The Saturday of No

Saturday morning raindrops
pelt the slate rooftop,
tap out a message
I don't want to hear:
No sunshine.
No clear blue.
No hopscotch.
No soccer.
No softball.
No skip rope.

Nope.

There goes my perfect day!
Bear-like, I growl about
the fun I'll miss.
My nose against
the windowpane,
I curse the rain,
then—wait!
I catch the storm's apology:
sun-drenched strips of color
arch across the sky—

  A rainbow!
  Oh! My!

— *Nikki Grimes*

RAINBOWS

Rainbows are created when sunlight passes through rain droplets in the sky. The light is broken up, or "refracted," into the seven colors of the visible spectrum: red, orange, yellow, green, blue, indigo, and violet.

Sometimes sunlight is refracted within clouds, which are called "rainbow clouds" because of their beautiful colors. This is called cloud iridescence, and it occurs most frequently in arctic regions.

Want to make your own rainbow? Spray a garden hose or sprinkler while facing away from the sun, and watch a rainbow appear!

PARHELIA

What happens when sunlight refracts through ice crystals, rather than through rain droplets? Sun dogs appear!

Sun dogs are also known as "mock suns," and they can be seen on either side of the sun (rather than opposite the sun, where rainbows appear). Though they aren't quite as colorful as rainbows, they can be very, very bright. Sun dogs form in clouds that are high up in the sky—most often cirrus or cirrostratus clouds.

Sun Dogs

Playful silver puppies
chasing tails
around, around;
circling December sky
but never touching ground.

                Heeling to their master
                        for a minute,
                            then away
they disappear to dance again
             another winter's day.

— *Matt Forrest Esenwine*

Hello, Pilot!

Can you see me
from your tiny window
in the eye
of your sly silver bird?
I trace circles around your shadow
as you nudge and smudge the clouds,
snug in my halo of rainbow light.
I delight in your wingtips
tickling my rings
red, yellow, indigo, green.
I am your optical escort,
born of water, clouds, sun—
a miracle of deflection,
I encircle your reflection.

Look at us here,
mirrored in the air—
soaring together
to who knows where!

— Renée M. LaTulippe

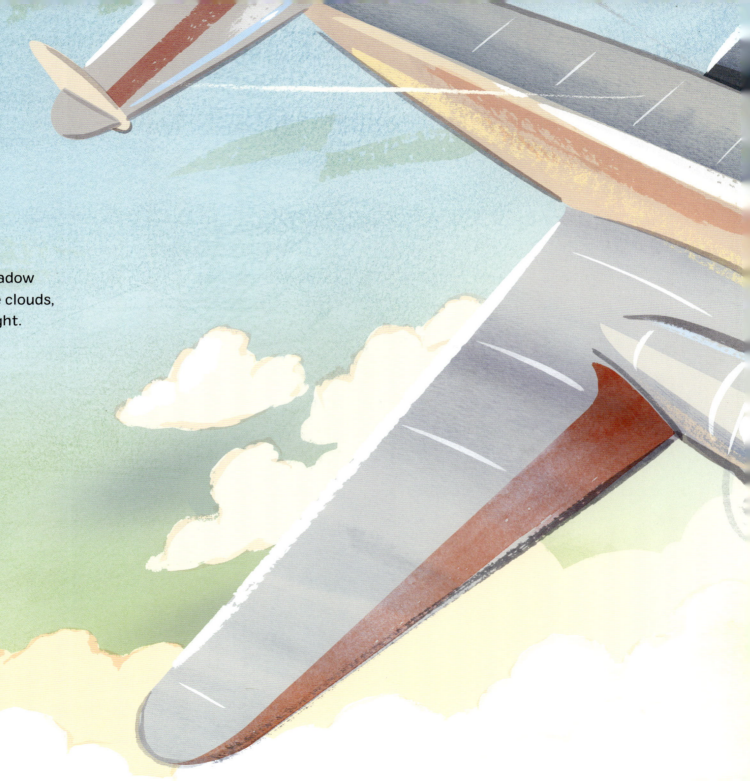

PILOT'S GLORIES

A "pilot's glory" or "pilot's halo" is a ring-shaped rainbow that occurs when sunlight is refracted in the water droplets of a cloud or heavy fog, rather than in drops of rain.

Pilot's glories get their name from the fact that they are often seen by people traveling in airplanes because they are above the cloud layer. But if you are in a tall building or mountain climbing, you might also see a glory! All it takes is water droplets in front of you and the sun at your back—which is why shadows usually accompany glories.

MOONBOWS

A moonbow is like a nighttime rainbow, occurring when moonlight (the sun's light, reflected off the surface of the moon) shines through rain or mist. This rare phenomenon happens only when the moon is full, and either just rising or setting.

A moonbow appears white to the naked eye; its prism of colors can only be seen in long-exposure photographs. One place to catch a moonbow is in the mist over Victoria Falls, a spectacular waterfall along the Zambezi River between Zambia and Zimbabwe in southern Africa.

Along the Zambezi

This dancer will not leap for long
over the span of Victoria Falls.
Thunderous water plunges down,
mist swirls up in silver shawls.

Over the span of Victoria Falls,
a full moon crowns the darkened hill.
Mist swirls up in silver shawls,
bending moonlight's slanting spill.

A full moon crowns the darkened hill.
Moonbow arches, ghostly white,
bending moonlight's slanting spill,
color hidden in its light.

Moonbow arches, ghostly white,
thunderous water plunges down.
Color hidden in its light,

The Rainbow Keeper

There's a girl who loves brilliant things:
crystals, gemstones, diamond rings.
She digs them up, wipes them clean.
She asks them: *what wonders have you seen?*
She marvels at their varied colors—
periwinkle, lime, cyan, butter.
She sings to them of geometry, of heat.
She displays them on her bedroom window seat.
Crystals are her favorite find—
especially the broken kind.
Their way of speaking is to glimmer,
shimmer, *SHINE!*
How do they make their tiny rainbows?
Only the Rainbow Keeper knows.

— Irene Latham

PRISMS AND CRYSTALS

Imagine carrying around a rainbow in your pocket! Just like water droplets and ice, some gems and other types of crystals can act as prisms if they have long, clear angles. They refract white light into the seven visible colors of the spectrum, and a rainbow appears.

Alexandrite, diamonds, and quartz are particularly effective at refracting sunlight into rainbows. You could hang one of these crystals in a window, and create your very own rainbow!

Reflections on the Pool

Miracle of nature at its best,
Blessed with bacteria tinted blue,
A clue for how the Glory got its hue.
Few geyser pools were ever better dressed.

Those first to see its beauty gazed in awe
At what they saw, this blue, inspiring spring,
A fragile thing, yet some around the ring
Would fling coins in the pool without a flaw.

Today we wish they'd left the pool alone.
Objects thrown, in spite of good intents,
Made poor sense and clogged hot water vents.
Had they no hints? Shouldn't they have known?

Morning Glory's blue faded fast,
Recast in yellow-green, too ruined to mend.
We can't defend how humans caused the end.
Nature must depend on us to last.

— *David L. Harrison*

MORNING GLORY POOL

This hot spring in Yellowstone National Park is an example of what happens when humans don't take care of their environment. Its original color was blue, due to bacteria that thrived in its hot waters. However, this pool is developing into a pool of rainbow colors—though not for positive reasons! Over the past hundred years, visitors have tossed coins, rocks, and garbage into the pool, lowering its temperature and adding other types of bacteria that are overtaking the original bacteria and causing the hot spring to lose some of its vivid blue color.

GRAND PRISMATIC SPRING

Yellowstone National Park is also home to Grand Prismatic Spring, which is similar to Morning Glory Pool in many ways, with its own sort of rainbow!

Larger than a football field, this giant hot spring also gets its rainbow of colors from various types of heat-loving bacteria living at different depths in the spring.

The spring's deep blue center is caused by the way it reflects blue color while absorbing all the other colors. This is also why the sky appears blue! And it's true for any color we see—the red edges of this spring absorb every color except red, reflecting that color back so our eyes see this area as red.

Sing the Life Prismatic

The science is easy—
boiling mineral water
bubbling up
from deep underground,
so hot you could make tea.
Add bacteria
in unreal pigments
plus microbes
that glow the color of fire
as they spill out
evenly on flattened ground
like the rays
of a mythical sun.

The poetry is harder to explain.
You could stare
into Earth's core,
through her fierce
crystal blue eye
swearing to make right

what was done—
clear-cutting,
oil-drilling,
deforestation—
all in the name of progress.
Or stir the fiery witch's cauldron,
promising your firstborn
to make her laugh
so her anger cools.

There is a poem here,
a fairy tale,
that mixes hope with color,
pride with promise,
science with mystery,
rapture with rainbow
ready to be spoken
to a broken world.

— *Heidi E.Y. Stemple & Jane Yolen*

Alien Fountain

Your mouth agape—steam and vapors
shooting up, up from deep within
an earthen belly, face rainbow-
stained with life—I stare,
wondering if, perhaps,
somewhere on some
far-distant planet,
there is anything
as spellbinding,
powerful,
beautiful
as a lone
peculiar
accident
that could
only have
been created
by human
ignorance
and Nature's
resilient
soul.

— *Matt Forrest Esenwine*

FLY GEYSER

Fly Geyser was created by accident in the 1960s when an energy company drilled into Nevada's Black Rock Desert searching for hot geothermal water. They found it . . . but since it was not hot enough for their purposes, they sealed it up.

Mother Nature doesn't always appreciate these sorts of things, though, and the geyser eventually opened up in several places, spewing out hot water and calcium carbonate. The calcium carbonate creates limestone, which formed larger and larger cone-shaped mounds, providing a perfect environment for algae to thrive. These algae create vibrant colors, creating a rainbow-like effect and giving the geyser its otherworldly appearance.

Caño Cristales Speaks

I'm a river in a rainbow.
I'm a rainbow in a river.
I ran away from Paradise.
(Or so do some believe.)

I glow in red and golden hues
but half the year I'm greens and blues.
I am a simple river
with a secret up my sleeve.

Color!

Today I'm rainbow poured in water.
Soon I will again be plain
magnificent and ordinary
as I carry crystal rain.

We each are much more than we seem.
Allow yourself, my child, to dream.

— *Amy Ludwig VanDerwater*

CAÑO CRISTALES

Located in Serranía de la Macarena National Park, in Colombia, South America, Caño Cristales is also known as "The River of Five Colors" or "The Liquid Rainbow." This river is like no other in the world: in between the hot, dry season and the cooler, wet season, when conditions are just right, the river blooms into color!

This is due to aquatic weeds reproducing in its waters. These plants cannot thrive when it's too hot or too wet, so during most of the year the river looks like any other river. But for a few short weeks in late spring and late autumn, the river flows with rainbows of vegetation!

Living Rainbows

Echoes of Rain

With open branches the tree
embraces the rain up high,
yellow, blue, violet dripping.
A rainbow is passing by.

Raindrops caught on branches
along the trunk slide down,
leaving echoes of color
that are welcomed by brown.

No one color will be missing
on the eucalyptus tree;
no one color will be missing
in the friends I want to see.

— *Alma Flor Ada &
F. Isabel Campoy*

RAINBOW EUCALYPTUS TREES

Found mostly in the islands of the South Pacific such as the Philippines, Indonesia, Papua New Guinea, and even the state of Hawaii, rainbow eucalyptus trees are quite possibly the most colorful tree you'll ever see!

As rainbow eucalyptus trees age, their brown bark peels off in strips, revealing a yellow-green pith underneath. Once this pith is exposed to air, it goes through a variety of color changes—showing off green, red, orange, and sometimes even purple streaks—before returning to its original brown.

RAINBOW LORIKEET

Can you imagine not enjoying the beauty of a rainbow-colored bird? There are many people who don't!

While rainbow lorikeets have striking, multicolored feathers that help attract potential mates and allow them to blend in among colorful rainforest plants, they are also often considered pests. These colorful birds can be noisy and aggressive—and they have taken over the habitat of many native bird species in parts of Australia and New Zealand. Farmers are especially annoyed because the birds can destroy apple, cherry, and other fruit crops.

Lament of the Fruit Farmer

Rainbow lorikeets are bothersome pests!
Don't be charmed by their plumage—it's a ruse.
Their attitude will put you to the test.
Rainbow lorikeets are bothersome pests!
They ransacked my trees like greedy guests
bedecked in grand, celestial hues.
Rainbow lorikeets are bothersome pests!
Don't be charmed by their plumage—it's a ruse.

— *Charles Waters*

Rainbows in a Cage

They wanted rainbows in a cage:
finches stolen from the wild.
A different time, a different age.
They wanted rainbows in a cage.
Capturing them was all the rage
for collectors whom those birds beguiled.
They wanted rainbows in a cage:
finches stolen from the wild.

— *Marilyn Singer*

GOULDIAN FINCH

In the mid-1800s, British bird expert John Gould named this Australian bird the "Lady Gouldian Finch" for his wife. Also known as the rainbow finch, these birds commonly have black, green, red, yellow, and purple feathers. Some even have blue, silver, or mauve colorings.

As these beautiful creatures became more widely known, more and more people began wanting them for pets—and the demand for Gouldian finches became so great they were nearly trapped and caged out of existence. Once abundant in the wild, the Gouldian finch is now a near-threatened species, meaning they could become endangered soon.

RAINBOW HIBISCUS

There are hundreds of varieties of hibiscus plants in the world. They come in every color of the rainbow, and some varieties even have multiple colors in one bloom—creating a little sliver of a rainbow on each petal. Hibiscus species come in a range of sizes, too, with flowers from two or three inches wide to nearly twelve inches wide!

While most hibiscus plants grow in warm, tropical climates, there are many that grow in areas of the United States—in the southeast, as well as Hawaii and southern California.

Petals of Paradise

Born of some wayward seed,
indeed a one-bloom bouquet
of rolled petals
tenderly ruffled and wrapped
with lilac and lavender,
lemon and sky;
a skirted pinwheel
hemmed with a touch of paradise
and who knows how
or why.

— *Rebecca Kai Dotlich*

PEACOCK MANTIS SHRIMP

The peacock mantis shrimp doesn't just display lots of colors, it SEES lots of colors—up to ten times more colors than humans! We can see wavelengths of color ranging from red to violet, but this special shrimp can see colors beyond those wavelengths that we can't. Imagine what a rainbow must looks like to the peacock mantis shrimp!

This little shrimp is also impressively powerful, using its club-like front claws to deliver punches that move at the speed of a bullet and can break apart the shells of the mollusks it eats.

Elegant Danger

Captivating beauty
with radiant appeal.

An appetite of titans.

Attitude of steel.

Throughout the sea
there is no shell
her fateful blow can't pierce.

*Just because you're beautiful
doesn't mean you can't be fierce.*

— Matt Forrest Esenwine

The Rainbowfish . . .

shimmies through
a crystal lake,

so bright you do
a double take.

Fins aflutter, he
glimmers, glides, and

on his scales
a rainbow rides.

— *Laura Purdie Salas*

RAINBOWFISH

The rainbowfish is another beautiful creature from Australia, although they can also be found in New Guinea and Madagascar. There are several different species of rainbowfish, each one unique in its brightly colored patterns. These fish get their colors from their iridescent scales, which reflect sunlight. Male rainbowfish can even change their colors to attract females!

In their native freshwater habitats, rainbowfish love eating mosquitoes. Because they are small and typically calm, they have become very popular for home aquariums.

PEACOCK SPIDER

The peacock spider, also known as the rainbow spider, is named for the color patterns on the males' abdomens. There are more than 80 different species of peacock spiders. Although these spiders are found across Australia, you'll need a keen eye to spot one: these colorful creatures are small—the largest is only the size of a child's fingernail!

Peacock spiders are remarkable because the males display a deep iridescent rainbow of colors to attract females. This may be the first known example in nature of males using the entire spectrum of rainbow of colors to attract mates. The rainbow colorings are so special that humans are studying them to learn more about color technology.

Night Gem

You brushed against
Nature's palette,
carried your cloak
of many colors
like a lantern
into the dark
where the light
of rainbows
had never been—
till you stepped in.

You left your gray web,
climbed out of your world
to brighten
the dull corners
of our universe
with your radiant array
on full display,
with the fan of glory
you proudly wore—
like no one before.

Little gem of night,
may you continue your
journey across the land
beyond the touch
of human hand
into safe realms
beyond our reach,
beyond our breach,
may you strut like a star—
like the peacock you are.

— *Charles Ghigna*

Jewel of the Pasture

Glinting a metallic shine
like fresh off the assembly line,
your hard work ethic can't be beaten!
(No lunch for me, thanks—I've already eaten.)

— *Matt Forrest Esenwine*

RAINBOW SCARAB

These shiny, colorful creatures can be found across the United States, from the eastern states to the southwest. The different colors on these beetles are due to how light reflects off their exoskeletons. The gold, green, and blue colors reflect off the scarab when light shines on it, making its colors glisten.

These beetles are usually found in or near pastures where animals graze. One of the most widespread species of dung beetle in the world, rainbow scarabs play an important role in recycling waste and nutrients within their ecosystem by feeding on dung (animal poop) as well as by rolling the dung into balls that they then use to feed their baby grubs.

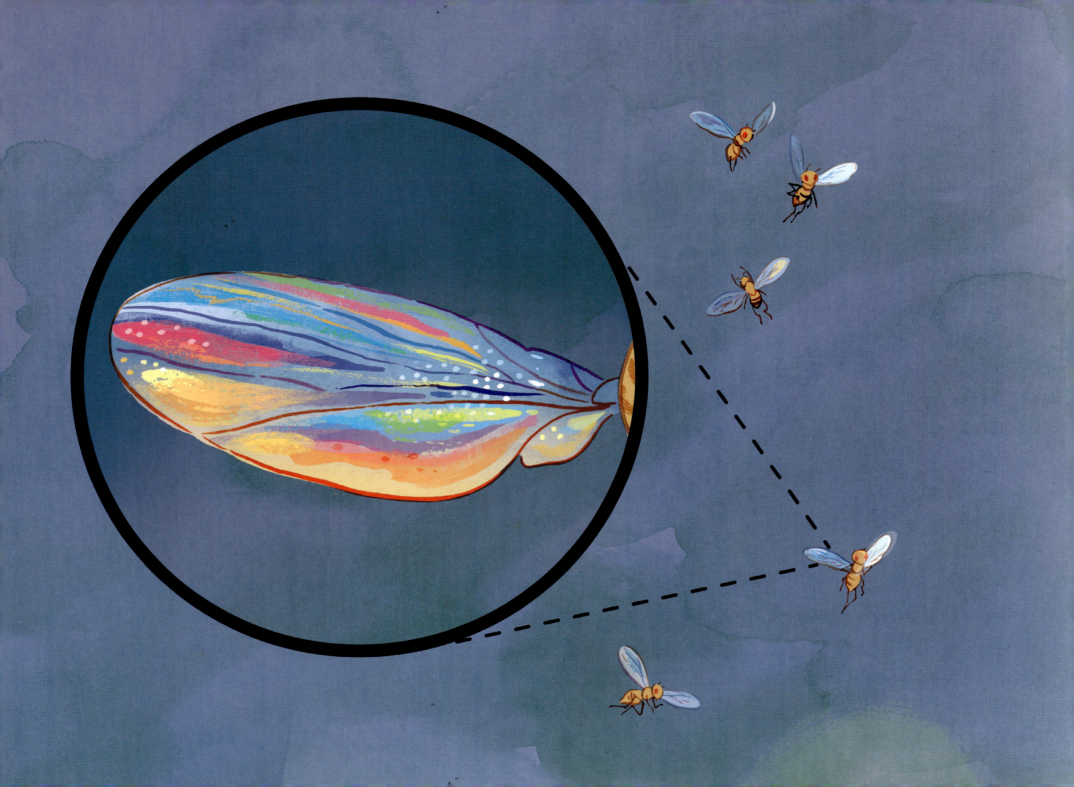

The Fruit Fly's Secret

Butterflies
get all the fuss—
in song,
art,
myth,
and news,
just because
they flit and flirt
on wings of rainbow hues.

"Torn love-notes,"
"Yellow symphonies,"
"Winged blossoms,"
poets laud.
"Ballet in the air"—or worse,
"Messengers of God."

Compared with them
I know
you think
I'm nothing
but a pest.
I breed in drains and sinks and mops.
I'm bland and underdressed.
I live to land on rotting pears,
ripe peaches,
cantaloupe.
And yet my wings boast rainbows, too—

    beneath a microscope!

— *Lee Wardlaw*

INSECT WINGS

In 2011, Swedish biologist Ekaterina Shevtsova discovered that the seemingly drab, transparent wings of fruit flies and wasps have a secret. When photographed (or examined under a microscope) against a black background, these insect wings reveal patterns of brilliant colors due to the way they refract light passing through them—just like a rainbow or prism. It turns out butterflies aren't the only insects with multicolored wings!

POEMS REFERENCED

Torn love-notes
— "The Genesis of Butterflies"
by Victor Hugo

Yellow symphonies
— "Symphony in Yellow"
by Oscar Wilde

Winged blossoms
— "Ode to a Butterfly"
by Thomas Wentworth Higginson

Ballet in the air
— Untitled Japanese haiku
by Bashō

Messengers of God
— "Messenger of God"
by Kathryn Poland

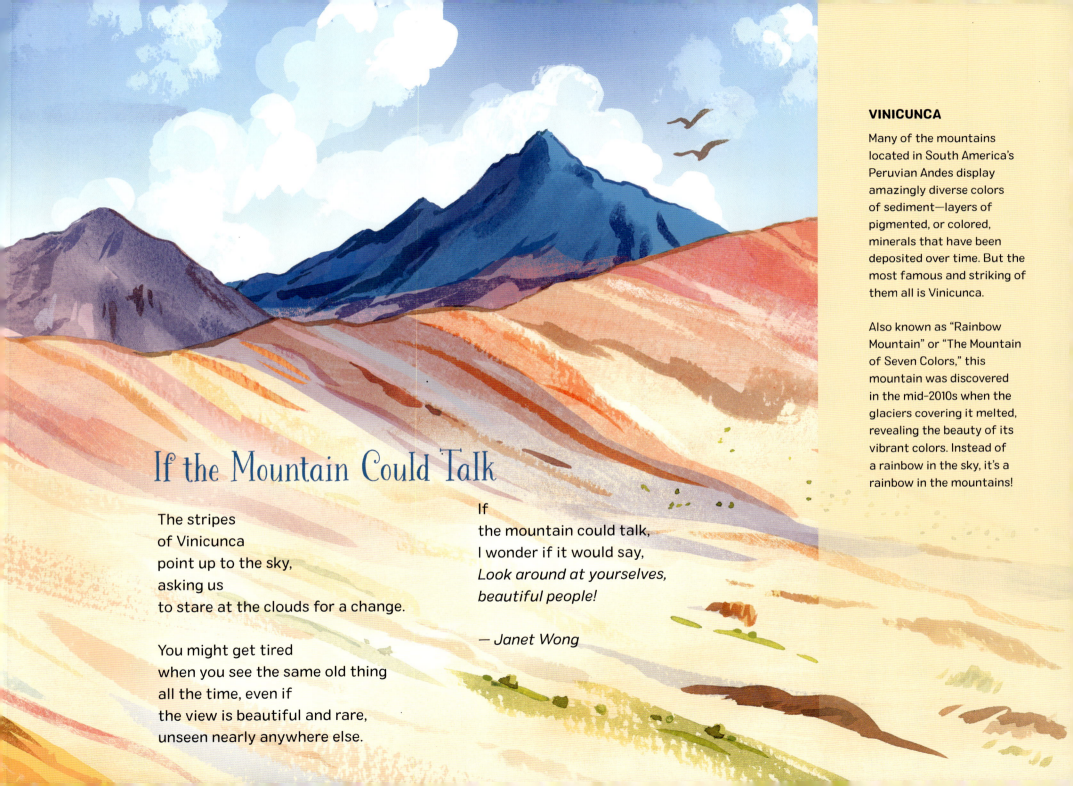

If the Mountain Could Talk

The stripes
of Vinicunca
point up to the sky,
asking us
to stare at the clouds for a change.

You might get tired
when you see the same old thing
all the time, even if
the view is beautiful and rare,
unseen nearly anywhere else.

If
the mountain could talk,
I wonder if it would say,
*Look around at yourselves,
beautiful people!*

— Janet Wong

VINICUNCA

Many of the mountains located in South America's Peruvian Andes display amazingly diverse colors of sediment—layers of pigmented, or colored, minerals that have been deposited over time. But the most famous and striking of them all is Vinicunca.

Also known as "Rainbow Mountain" or "The Mountain of Seven Colors," this mountain was discovered in the mid-2010s when the glaciers covering it melted, revealing the beauty of its vibrant colors. Instead of a rainbow in the sky, it's a rainbow in the mountains!

What We Left in Rainbow Cave

Climb into the poet's waiting boat.
Then float across Carrera Lake
and make your way to Rainbow Cave,
carved by time and azure wave.
Now enter sun-shot gaps and gasp.
Be still and wait. And watch the shafts
of sunlight shine through water blue
and shatter into dazzling hues
that dance on glistening marble walls.
Now listen to the echoed calls
of swifts that flutter rainbow air.
If only we could join them there, we say.
Then from below, the silver fish
give answer to our whispered wish:
"No matter if you've gone away
some part of you will always stay,
with swift and fish and azure wave,
inside the heart of Rainbow Cave."

— *Allan Wolf*

LAS CAVERNAS DE MÁRMOL

How can something that is white be so colorful? At the southernmost tip of South America, in an area known as Patagonia (which is shared by Argentina and Chile), you will find Cuevas de Mármol (the Cave), Catedral de Mármol (the Cathedral), and Capillas de Mármol (the Chapel), known collectively as Las Cavernas de Mármol, or the Marble Caves. These caves formed naturally thousands of years ago from 300-million-year-old calcium carbonate mineral deposits, and continue to change through weathering and erosion.

Although the caves are mostly white marble with some light pink and blue coloration, the formations reflect the sunlight that is refracting off the blue glacial waters of General Carrera Lake. The rainbow colors seen can vary greatly depending on the time of day, the level of the lake water, and the seasons.

World Beneath Our Feet

Mountains rise, await
our footsteps; we are as gods
walking on rainbows

—Matt Forrest Esenwine

ZHANGYE DANXIA NATIONAL GEOPARK

These brightly colored mountains, sometimes called "The Rainbow Mountains," can be found in the foothills of the Qilian Mountains, in China's Zhangye Danxia National Geopark. They took millions of years to form, as quartz, iron, and other multicolored minerals were deposited over time and eventually turned into sandstone and siltstone. These rocks became twisted and crumpled due to shifts in the Earth's crust as the Himalayan mountain range formed, and then wind and rain sculpted the mountains into the shapes we see today. Walking on rainbows, indeed!

Garden of Stars

In a celestial nursery,
cosmic clouds of dust
tend a dimming star—
sprouts of rainbow powder burst:
lilac, rose, blue aster . . .
a blooming bouquet

light years away.

— *Georgia Heard*

RAINBOW NEBULA

A massive, swirling cloud of gas surrounds the dying star Betelgeuse, a red supergiant a thousand times larger than our sun. As it ages, the star sheds material that collects around it, creating what is known as a nebula. The different types of gases and dust in the nebula cause it to appear as a rainbow of colors—and those colors in turn help scientists know what gases are in the nebula.

Don't confuse the Rainbow Nebula with the Orion Nebula, though—while Betelgeuse can be seen as one of Orion's shoulders, the Orion Nebula is a completely different nebula just below Orion's belt. New stars are slowly being born in both nebulas at this very moment!

Recommended Resources

BOOKS

Find a copy of the following books to learn more about how rainbows work and how they show up in our world:

Davis, Rachael. *Over the Rainbow: The Science, Magic, and Meaning of Rainbows*. Illus. by Wenjia Tang. London: Flying Eye Books, 2023.

Jameson, Karen. *Time to Shine: Celebrating the World's Iridescent Animals*. Illus. by Dave Murray. Toronto: Groundwood Books, 2022.

Kanani, Sheila. *Can You Get Rainbows in Space? A Colorful Compendium of Space and Science*. London: Puffin Books, 2023.

Wick, Walter. *A Ray of Light*. New York: Scholastic, 2019.

WEBSITES

Check out the following websites to find pictures and learn more about each of the rainbows you've read about:

Rainbows

National Geographic Education, "Rainbow"
education.nationalgeographic.org/resource/rainbow/

Parhelia

Space.com, "What Are Sundogs and How Do They Form?"
space.com/sundogs-definition-formation-science

Pilot's Glories

Nasa Earth Observatory, "Glory of the Pilot"
earthobservatory.nasa.gov/blogs/earthmatters/2018/07/09/glory-of-the-pilot/

Moonbows

Almanac.com, "What Is a Moonbow?"
almanac.com/moonbows

Prisms and Crystals

Sciencing, "How Do Prisms Work?"
sciencing.com/prisms-work-4965588.html

Morning Glory Pool

Smithsonian Magazine, "Tourist Trash Has Changed the Color of Yellowstone's Morning Glory Pool"
smithsonianmag.com/smart-news/tourist-trash-has-changed-color-yellowstones-morning-glory-pool-180954239/

Grand Prismatic Spring

Smithsonian Magazine, "The Science Behind Yellowstone's Rainbow Hot Spring"
smithsonianmag.com/travel/science-behind-yellowstones-rainbow-hot-spring-180950483/

Fly Geyser

GeologyScience, "The Fly Geyser, USA"
geologyscience.com/gallery/geological-wonders/the-fly-geyser-usa/

Caño Cristales

GeologyScience, "The Caño Cristales River, Colombia"
geologyscience.com/gallery/geological-wonders/the-cano-cristales-river-colombia/

Rainbow Eucalyptus Trees

Science Friday, "Rainbow in a Tree"
sciencefriday.com/articles/rainbow-in-a-tree/

Rainbow Hibiscus

San Diego Zoo Wildlife Alliance, "Hibiscus"
animals.sandiegozoo.org/plants/hibiscus

Gouldian Finch

Animalia, "Gouldian Finch"
animalia.bio/gouldian-finch

Rainbow Lorikeet

Animalia, "Rainbow Lorikeet"
animalia.bio/rainbow-lorikeet

Peacock Mantis Shrimp

PBS, "Peacock Mantis Shrimp Fact Sheet"
pbs.org/wnet/nature/blog/peacock-mantis-shrimp-fact-sheet/

Rainbowfish

The Spruce Pets, "25 Colorful Species of Rainbowfish"
thesprucepets.com/types-of-rainbow-fish-5272300

Peacock Spider

UC San Diego Today, "Nature's Smallest Rainbows, Produced by Peacock Spiders, May Inspire New Optical Technologies"
today.ucsd.edu/story/natures_smallest_rainbows_produced_by_peacock_spiders_may_inspire_new_optic

Rainbow Scarab

University of Florida Extension, "Rainbow Scarab"
edis.ifas.ufl.edu/publication/IN1003

Insect Wings

National Geographic, "Wasps and Flies Have Hidden Rainbows in Their Wings"
nationalgeographic.com/science/article/forget-butterflies-wasps-and-flies-have-hidden-rainbows-in-their-wings

Vinicunca

GeologyIn, "The Rainbow Mountains in Peru—Vinicunca"
geologyin.com/2016/02/the-rainbow-mountains-in-peru-very.html

Las Cavernas de Mármol

GeologyScience, "The Marble Caves"
geologyscience.com/gallery/geological-wonders/the-marble-caves/

Zhangye Danxia National Geopark

GeologyScience, "Zhangye Danxia Landform or Rainbow Mountains"
geologyscience.com/gallery/geological-wonders/zhangye-danxia-landform-or-rainbow-mountains

Rainbow Nebula

Space.com, "Supergiant Star's Rainbow Nebula Revealed"
space.com/12051-bright-nebula-photo-supergiant-star-betelgeuse.html

Glossary

Bacteria: Single-celled organisms that were some of the first forms of life to evolve on Earth. Nearly all bacteria can only be seen with a microscope. Certain types of bacteria thrive in high temperatures like those found in hot springs—these are referred to as thermophilic ("heat-loving") bacteria.

Calcium Carbonate: One of the major components of limestone, this is a naturally-occurring type of white salt that can be used for a variety of reasons, from helping relieve upset stomachs to marking lines on athletic fields!

Climate: The type of long-term weather and temperature of a particular area.

Ecosystem: An environment where a group of living creatures exist and interact with each other.

Electromagnetic Spectrum: The electromagnetic spectrum is the full range of electromagnetic energy moving through our universe in waves. The light we can see is only a small part of this spectrum. Human eyes can see a range of seven colors (red, orange, yellow, green, blue, indigo, and violet) that make up the visible spectrum of light, but there are many **wavelengths** of electromagnetic energy on this spectrum that are invisible to us, like infrared or ultraviolet light.

Endangered: At risk of becoming **extinct** in the near future due to risk factors like habitat loss, climate change, poaching, or invasive species.

Exoskeleton: A hard covering on the outside of an animal that protects and supports its body.

Extinct: Pertaining to a group or family of creatures that no longer exists.

Geothermal: Pertaining to, or related to, the Earth's internal heat.

Geyser: Water that comes into contact with magma (hot, molten rock) under the Earth's surface, heats to boiling, and erupts through the ground in a burst of hot water and steam.

Iridescence: A colorful appearance that shifts with movement or viewing angle, caused by specific ways that light waves are **refracted** by certain surfaces like soap bubbles or butterfly wings.

Minerals: Nonliving substances that occur naturally and make up the rocks, sand, and soil found on Earth.

Mollusk: A member of "Mollusca," a group of invertebrate (having no internal skeleton) animals that includes snails, squids, clams, scallops, nudibranchs, and about 100,000 other species!

Phenomenon: An observable event or situation that is often unusual or surprising.

Pigment: A material that gives color to whatever it is part of because of the way it reflects or absorbs certain **wavelengths** of light.

Pith: The soft, light-colored part of a tree, beneath the bark, where new cells grow.

Reflection: When a ray of light approaches a surface and bounces back, rather than being absorbed or **refracted**.

Refraction: A beam of light might appear white, but it's actually made up of all the visible colors of the **electromagnetic spectrum**. When that white light hits an object like a raindrop or a prism, it is bent or refracted, scattering the light and separating it out into distinct colors.

Transparent: Clear, or clear enough, to allow light to completely pass through.

Wavelength: Electromagnetic energy, including visible light, moves in waves that have varying lengths, or frequencies. Red light has a longer wavelength than blue light, for instance. Radio waves have the longest wavelength on the **electromagnetic spectrum**, while gamma rays have the shortest wavelength.